Novice

poems by

Pamela Rasso

Finishing Line Press
Georgetown, Kentucky

Novice

Copyright © 2017 by Pamela Rasso
ISBN 978-1-63534-210-9 First Edition
All rights reserved under International and Pan-American Copyright Conventions.
No part of this book may be reproduced in any manner whatsoever without written permission from the publisher, except in the case of brief quotations embodied in critical articles and reviews.

ACKNOWLEDGMENTS

Grateful acknowledgment is made to the editors and staff of the following publications in which these poems first appeared:

"Three Weeks with Etheridge Knight." *Rattle*. Volume 20, Number 1, Spring 2014.
"The Man Who Lived in a Box." *Oberon Poetry Magazine*. Fourteenth Annual Issue. 2016.

Publisher: Leah Maines

Editor: Christen Kincaid

Cover Art: Monica Gambacorto

Author Photo: Jocelyn Steiber

Cover Design: Elizabeth Maines McCleavy

Printed in the USA on acid-free paper.
Order online: www.finishinglinepress.com
also available on amazon.com

Author inquiries and mail orders:
Finishing Line Press
P. O. Box 1626
Georgetown, Kentucky 40324
U. S. A.

Table of Contents

Fire Island Ferries 1

All Ears 2

The Substitute 3

Learning to Drive 4

Race Riot 5

First Steps on the Carousel 6

Lay, Lady, Lay 8

Making Dinner for Robert Hayden 9

On Becoming 10

The Legend of the One Handed Princess 11

Three Weeks with Etheridge Knight 13

33 Greene 14

Having To Make a Living. Somehow 16

The Man Who Lived in a Box 17

Gluttons for Poetry 18

Immigrant's Song 19

Thanksgiving Dinner 20

The Little Toy Boy 21

My Mentor, Marsha Tucker 22

Debut 23

To Bryce, Nicolette and Kieran

Fire Island Ferries

Growing up on the south shore of Long Island in the 1960's was a paradise in the summertime for children. We would take the ferries to Fire Island. Watch Hill. Davis Park. Old Inlet. Fireplace. Ocean Beach. There we would swim, body surf, watch with amazement the mating of horseshoe crabs, the razor clams as they erected straight up then buried themselves in the wet sand, collected sea shells, skate cases, watched and fed the herring gulls. There were some ferries, for reasons we did not understand, that we were not allowed on. Mischievously, one day my brother, Mr. Diavolo himself, whispered to me that he and his friends were going to take the forbidden ferry and I tagged along with them. It was the ferry to Cherry Grove. Why was it that parents did not want their children going there? The very name, Cherry Grove, sounded so beautiful to me. It summoned up visions of cherry trees, pink blossoms cascading in the wind, delicate petals covering the sand. Once there we hid like thieves. Then we started laughing. There was a man dressed in a woman's bikini. Why was he dressed in woman's clothing? We saw a man holding hands with another man. Other men grasping each other in embraces. Men kissing each other on the lips. We snuck back home bewildered by what we had seen.

All Ears

Late one evening, when my brothers and sisters were asleep, I heard noises from the bathroom. Mother and father were in the shower together. I heard the rhythmic streams of water pouring from the shower head. I heard a duet of soprano songs and tenor songs. I heard mother laughing and giggling, sizzling in the hot rippling water. I heard my father grunt, grunt, grunt. I heard the earthy noises, gasps of breath like those taken by the drowning. The squeals, moans, snorts, mewing, roaring, cooing, howling, singing, humming, whimper. Silence then except for the tap tap tapping of the drops of water. Mother and father. Why were they making such noises?

The Substitute

The dark eyed beauty with the secretive eyes. She was always very shy in school. She never talked with anyone. As we grew up we never went to play at her home.

The dark eyed beauty with the sorrowful eyes. Thin and shapely. She was the oldest daughter. She looked just like her mother. Everyone said so.

The dark eyed beauty with the pain in her eyes. We didn't understand. Till one day the fist of her father pulverized and closed

her dark crouching eyes.

Learning to Drive

Rat man, my brother, and his friends Maff and Ash Can offered to take me out driving to give me some pointers as I was learning how to drive. Rat Man had an old, rusty, red Chevelle with what his friends called "awesome" tires. Maff took the wheel while I sat next to him. Rat Man and Ash Can in the back seat. Maff jerked out the driveway in reverse then slammed on the accelerator riding on the neighbors lawns etching imprints, clipping aluminum garbage cans that fell down one after the other as if he was a knight jousting on a horse leaving his opponents all dead on the ground.

Soon Maff was accelerating as we went faster and faster. He lifted his hands off the steering wheel saying "Look at me!" laughing, squealing gleefully as I screamed. He was rickracking from side to side in the lane speeding up, slowing down, speeding up. The boys all leaned back trying to pop wheelies as I yelled "Stop. Stop you stupid broncos," while they continued laughing. Next they started car dancing round and round and round. 360. Pirouettes. I was giddy dizzy terrified. Next they all leaned in the direction of the driver's side trying to car ski on 2 wheels. I was thrown smack into Maff. I screeched like a female red fox. "You're going to kill us. We're going to roll over. Stop. Stop," as Rat Man and Ash Can opened the windows on the other side sticking their reckless heads out in the onrushing wind. "We're going to die. I'm going to die. Stop I'm going to die." And it seemed as if the car took off the 2 wheels for a moment into the air ascending beyond the clouds delirium death star rush thrill blaze while I gasped and then it fell back to the earth with and thump and drove on.

"Stop the car. I want to get out. Stop the car immediately" I demanded. "Ah Lucy van Pelt," Rat Man said," Chill out. Maff is just showing off. He likes you."

Race Riot

It started at the bonfire. In the darkness an army of older Black kids came running out of the woods. One had a gun. Was it real or an authentic looking child's toy? Was it loaded? The parking lot. Fighting. White kids. Black kids. Running into the gymnasium to get bats. The Black kids yelling "Malcolm X. Malcolm X." The white kids yelling "Stop. Stop." The Black boy pulling swatches of hair from the head of the pretty white girl. Beat her up. The white kids retaliating. "The Red Coats are coming. The Red Coats are coming." Everyone scattering. The next day in school the DA's (Dunton Avenue Gang) couldn't go into the bathrooms without a fight. The Black girl whacked the straight A white girl on the head with the lacrosse stick pummeling her to the ground. The Bay kids screaming "Give us back our school." The Black kids screaming "It's not YOUR school. We want Black teachers. We want Black history." The PR's screaming "We demand Puerto Rican studies." The Swamp Rats said "Stop destroying the school. Education is key." The Black girl wearing a big tooth comb in her hair like war gear threw the white woman teacher down the stairs. "Black Power." "White Power." Police. Black students being padlocked. "Why are only Black students being padlocked?" the intelligent Black girl demanded. The principal on the loud speaker screaming "Get outta here. Get outta here. Go home. Go home." Walking the long 7 miles home from Beaver Dam Road to South Country Shores. My sister crying. My brother smoking pot.

First Steps on the Carousel

Late spring. 1970. Nixon had invaded Cambodia. Marches in Washington. The draft. Innocent students massacred by the National Guard at Kent State. A serious time. We had shut the colleges down. Triumph. I had met a young man named Tee. He was tall and thin with long, long hair. Tee had some notoriety. He had sewn the American flag to the seat of his pants. He had been suspended from his Virginia college for his rebellious activities. Newspapers carried the story of the young man who had sewn the American flag to the seat of his pants. He was threatened with court suits. He talked defiantly about going all the way to the Supreme Court.

Visiting Long Island Tee and I were walking slowly, close to each other at the beach at Smith's Point collecting sea shells, talking about the war in Vietnam, about feminism, about oppression. As it grew darker we made a campfire. Tee had brought his guitar and was playing folk music serenading me by the flames. So perfect. He had brought several bottles of wine, the kind that adolescents drink, Boone's Farm Strawberry Hill. I had always thought alcohol was so romantic like in the Hollywood films. "Here's looking at you kid!" Humphrey Bogart toasts to the beauteous Ingrid Bergman or William Powell and Myrna Loy drunkenly bantering wittily back and forth. I drank and drank and drank the cheapo wine that tasted like strawberry soda. So romantic. Behaving like an adult. I wanted to feel what it felt like to be intoxicated. One minute I was singing with the guitar the next I was stepping out on to the carousel smiling and laughing swirling and swirling, music, wine, Tee, romance, horses, tigers, lions, unicorns, giraffes, Cinderella's couch, me free alone with Tee, the ocean, the flames, the stars.

Then I spewed all over Tee, his guitar, the fire, me. Vomit all over. I tried to cover up the puke with sand. Tee picked me up, threw me and himself into the ocean that cleansed us of my dinner.

Plopping me onto the couch in my parent's house Tee told my inquisitive mother that he was returning me because I was a dangerous date. My mother, upset, ran round and round the house screaming "I'm so ashamed of you. I'm so ashamed of you" "Why?" Tee asked. He continued "In my whole life I have never witnessed such a delicate, elegant, classy, graceful barf!"

Lay, Lady, Lay

Circles of candles flickering in the night in a dorm room. Wine. An altar. The man plays his guitar and sings of the lady on his bed from a Bob Dylan song. The lady is glistening like the gold in a painting by Giotto. The Madonna. She begins to recite a passage from Molly Bloom, the one about the Magic Mountain and yes yes yes. He continues with a song by Donovan, the one about Guinevere rustling around the castle in white velvet, silk and lace. He tells her she is an enchantress, the woman he has most desired in his entire life. He tells her she is beautiful, from a noble Roman family. He runs his fingers down her long dark hair. She runs her fingers down his long, dark hair. She sings with him. A duet of the shimmering. Heat rises. She hears the thunderous noise of a jousting knight on a horse. She thinks his penis is magnificent, a horse penis, a spire, a colossus. He calls her Guinevere of the labyrinth mind, secrets in every corridor. She is the lady in gold in a Klimt painting. He has stopped singing, the guitar placed down on the side of the brass bed but the man and the woman both hear the singing go on and on in their hearts as they rustle, velvet and lace and sparkle, ghosts in each other's corridors rising to the sun.

Making Dinner for Robert Hayden

With an earnest face I peeled the potatoes until they looked like little moons. I sliced the carrots, cubed the beef. It all had to be perfect for I was making dinner for Robert Hayden. Novice at the trade, I thought that I needed to make a dinner that was "haute cuisine," a dinner right out of the famous French cookbooks to be a dinner good enough for a great poet. The key to superb Boeuf Bourguignon Roger told me, was throwing one or two squares of fresh, unsweetened chocolate into the stew. He had heard this from a *hotesse, porte de Vanes*, who was an international *championne d'epee*. I lit the cognac, poured in the Bourguignon, the chocolate, set it all simmering. Best to be made the day before but as a student, I hadn't thought that far ahead. I served the concoction to Robert Hayden, who was delicate as a seahorse with thick penetrating big lens eyes. Shyly I glowed as he told me how delicious it was, mostly due to the advice of Roger. Afterwards we talked for hours about poetry, African art, about the wooden ceremonial masks made for the young women when they had their first blood letting, their rite of passage to womanhood. "You have much going against you being ethnic and a woman," he said. "But keep at it, poetry is within you." Over the years I have cooked many meals, become accomplished. But no meal was ever finer than my initiation dinner, the one for Robert Hayden.

On Becoming

It was a time when women poets were more unusual, the school year 1972-1973. A conference of high school and university teachers of English had invited the woman poet Muriel Rukeyser as the guest writer. Beginner poet, I was excited to hear a woman poet read. Looking at her from the audience, she had a looming, overpowering, lumberjack presence. Her face was not delicate, rather it was wide, earthy, turniplike. Her voice gruff. She had taken flying lessons when young. Her words flew around the room. She had gone to Hanoi, was against the war in Vietnam.

When her reading ended, I was startled. Muriel was sitting alone. No one was going up to her to sign books, no one was approaching her with warm smiles, praise, handshakes, congratulations, applause, gratefulness. Instead, indifference. Or worse. I listened. There was ridicule from some of the male poets. There was harshness from others. Criticism. There was hostility. Seeing her all alone I went up to her, sat down to talk with her. I told her which of the poems she had just read that I loved the most. The one where she asks her lover to speak to her, another that began "Yes, we were looking at each other." It reminded me of the Molly Bloom soliloquy from Ulysses I told her even though I don't think this is what she meant. She asked me if I wrote poetry. I nodded. We talked about being a young woman trying to write poetry. We chatted and laughed. It was then I knew. Being a woman poet meant taking your plane and flying it solo smack into the iridescent bubble of conventionality. It meant loneliness. Harshness. Hostility. Ridicule. Belittlement. Rejection. And yes, triumph. I knew then, this is what it was to be a woman poet.

The Legend of the One Handed Princess

Once upon a time there was a beautiful princess. But she had one flaw—she only had one hand. Where the other hand should have been there was only a nubby stub. She was intelligent, talented, joyous and hopeful. The handsome prince from the nearby kingdom fell in love with the beautiful princess from the first time his eyes met hers. He did not care that the princess was not perfect, that she had only one hand.

The prince would kiss the stubby nub that was her other hand. He would tell her over and over how much he loved her, how much he wanted to marry her.

His parents took him aside. They said "You can date her but you can never marry her for she has no hand."

One parent says "You cannot marry her, she's Italian." Another parent says "He's from the wrong side of the tracks." Another parent tells his son he cannot marry a woman because she is not Jewish. Another parent says he cannot marry her because she IS Jewish. "He's Black. What would the neighbors say?" "She's not intelligent enough." "She's too studious." "He doesn't have any money. He's poor."

The princess does not understand this. "Am I so repulsive?" she inquires. "Am I so hideous to your father the king and your mother the queen?"

The princess tells the prince to muster up some balls and tell his parents where to go.

The prince marries another princess from a different kingdom who has both hands.

The one handed princess is sad. She cries. She tries to make sense of the word "love." She curls up into a little ball and disappears into herself.

Soon the king dies. The prince inherits the kingdom and the crown.

Three Weeks with Etheridge Knight

The first time we met, Etheridge eyed me with suspicion, said "O a white picket fence white girl." And "White paper doll." He had been to prison. I told him I had never known anyone who had been to prison. He called me "Starch." He said he had snatched an old ladies pocketbook. I told him that stealing was wrong. He called me "White Sunday school teacher." He said he had been given 25 years for stealing an old ladies pocketbook. I agreed that was too harsh. He called everyone "Brother" and "Sister" such as "Brother Bill" and "Sister Sue." He said white girls flashed their shiny white thighs at him. He said he saw my white short shorts, tube top, white titties. He said was I trying to burn some coal? I told him I liked his Haiku very much, thought his poems were rough jolt raw red meat. He said "You dig my Haiku? You dig my Haiku. Wow. He called me "Smarty pink ass." He read my poems. I said growing up Italian wasn't so easy either. He said "O, Mafia white girl." I said "Exactly my point." He signed his book for me writing "The stars are free/& we gonna be/too." Then he called me "Refined white sugar." He called me "Top shelf woman."

33 Greene

Entering the lobby of 33 Greene Street in SoHo, NYC, 1976 there was an arrow pointing downward to the basement that read "Fallout shelter." Next to the sign was another that said "Beware of Dog." The word dog was crossed out, the word David inserted so the sign read "Beware of David."

This was my first year after graduate school in NYC where I was living in the old fallout shelter in the basement of the building. Descending downward in the dark, down Dantesque bowels of hell, suddenly there was what looked like a phantasmagoria, fantasy land, a magic world. There were paintings all around that reminded one of moonscapes, imaginary worlds, space, underwater, forests. This was the lair of the American abstract surrealist painter David Gregg. I once watched David paint nonstop for 3 days straight, smoking a jay, laughing as he stomped on and then delicately painted his visionary scenes on canvas. Next to him was a space inhabited by the artist and composer, Scott Johnson. Sometimes I would go to bed. When I awoke in the morning there was a large sculpture made of wood, plastic, rope and other assorted found discarded pieces by Scott. The next day there would be an entirely different sculpture in the same space and the next day another one. Constant change. Limitless sculptures made of the same wood, rope and plastic. Sometimes I would listen to Scott play his own compositions on his electric guitar sitting there in the middle of his most recent sculpture.

In one of the rooms was the playwright Lawrence Backstedt. Larry would read out loud to us his most recent plays, *The Saint Julia's Day Massacre, The Ballerina Plays Ball*. His wife Roseanne was a painter whose works combined the natural and the man made in an understated abstract realism. Larry and Roseanne were members of Aesthetic Realism and they tried relentlessly to convert us to the cause. Their little daughter Simone would dance around and around throughout the basement delighting everyone present. Above was Deborah Shaffer who had formed an all women's documentary cooperative. Often Charlie Moulton appeared. Charlie was a dancer in Merce Cunningham's dance troupe. He was a virtuoso tap dancer. Once David shined a spotlight on Charlie who danced for us. David called Charlie the "dainty elephant." I was the resident poet.

And we talked and we talked and we argued and argued. Ideas, thoughts and language ricocheting around. About politics. About the Ontological Hysteric Theater. About John Cage. About Laurie Anderson. About Art and Language or as we called the group "Art and Languish."About Artists Meeting For Cultural Change, other left wing political art groups, The Anti Catalog. David, Scott, Charlie and Larry played chess. There was a fierce rivalry going on, the score list kept on the wall. Once I watched Scott and Charlie engaged in a game of chess where they took candle wax forming clothing, hats, trousers, dresses, swords, breasts, vaginas and penises on the chess pieces. Sometimes we would all eat. Sometimes we had no money for food.

So much talent and creativity going on in a basement that most people would have thought of as bleak and uninhabitable.

Having To Make a Living. Somehow.

"Welcome aboard," the man who is to be my boss says shaking my hand. He drags me to meet the Senior Executive Vice President who concurs "Welcome aboard." Next I am shepherded from cubicle to cubicle where the employees look like jars of jam packed tightly in corrugated cardboard. Each person repeats the same words, "Welcome aboard." And then again "Welcome aboard." I hadn't realized I was embarking on a ship. Shyly, I shrink into my cubicle. Later in the day we are at a round table discussion. When asked I voice my opinion. My boss looks at me in horror. "You're so naïve. You have the idealism of a child." When I try to defend myself and protest this isn't so he blares "Justice is for idiots."

My boss comes into my cubicle. He picks up a book from my desk. "Dostoyevsky," he reads. "Don't bring books to work," he scolds me. He explains "It doesn't look good." He continues on "You are an amorphous shape that needs to fit into our square peg. Try harder." "Yes," I respond. There I am some Don Quixote thrusting imaginary lances, humming some bars to myself of *The Man from La Mancha*. I need to pay my rent. I wonder when did a word like idealism that should have been like multi colored helium balloons rising to the sky become a word tied with concrete bricks that needed to be thrown overboard plummeting to the ooze and muck of the sea bottom? I need food.

Late afternoon a man quietly comes into my cubicle. He softly whispers "I think you are quite a philosophical young woman." I smile, the first time that day. In the evening he and I go to The Film Anthology Archives to see *Au Hazard Balthazar*.

The Man Who Lived in a Box

Outside my building door there was a man who lived in a box. I don't know where he came from, he appeared as if from some darker place. The box, his home, was a large discarded cardboard box from an appliance such as a washing machine or stove left on the street for garbage by one of the residents of the lofts. He carried the box around on his shoulders, moving it now and then like a hermit crab seeking some comfortable, hospitable location.

I would walk past his residence and peek inside. There was a mattress, blankets, bags of small possessions. I could smell his home for some distance away, knowing it was there before I came to this block. I could hear him mumbling, talking to himself on matters, I think, of great importance to him. I had grown up on the Great South Bay of Long Island in a lovely neighborhood that had once been the southern gardens of the Durkee spice family estate with magnolias and osage orange. I had never before seen a man living in a box.

Everyone called him "homeless." But he had a "home."

I wondered if he had a family? I imagined he was a rejected lover or a deserted son, a once famous ballet dancer who could no longer dance, a rapist or an axe murderer from a scary movie. More likely he was mentally ill, alcoholic or a drug abuser. He lived outside my door through three seasons. Then, in the winter, in a snow storm, he disappeared.

Maybe he carried his home on his back over a heated subway grate, maybe he moved to a warmer, more hospitable climate. Maybe he was picked up by the police or a rescue squad and taken to a local flophouse. But most likely, he became an ice angel that night.

Gluttons for Poetry

The poet Jack Gilbert told me that when he was a young man he was so poor he would sleep on park benches and allow himself one chocolate bar a day for food. I heard Charles Simic also say that in the past he had been so poor he lived on one chocolate bar a day. Was this what it was to be a poet? At a poetry reading a woman poet said that in the 60's she gave blow jobs and turned tricks in Bryant Park for food. Once while walking on the Lower East Side I watched Allen Ginsberg dip his hand into a city garbage can and pull out some food which he greedily devoured.

Immigrant's Song

Juan came to America like countless others. He got a job as a building worker for one of the buildings in New York City. He could be paid lower wages because he was not a part of the union. Next he brought his wife and two little daughters to their new home in America. He worked very hard all day running the freight elevator, doing construction, maintenance, odd jobs, repairs. Around dusk he would climb to the rooftop of the building whose care had been entrusted to him. He would sit on the ledge, look out across the skyline at the glistening city that was becoming his own. The stars appeared and he felt he was up so high he could almost touch them. He thought the lights on the skyscrapers and bridges mirrored heaven. He felt he was a man of two parts, part of him in his native country, part of him in his new found paradise. He would spend hours and hours on the rooftop dreaming of his plans, his ambitions. His heart sang of his future, of America.

One day as Juan was fixing the elevator, Gino, Gino the Jinx as he was called, came in, turned the elevator on. Juan was sliced in half, two slabs of bloody red meat hanging in the ropes as if in a slaughter house. Instantly killed the medics said. But those of us who looked in the elevator could see the two parts swaying on the ropes, could hear a gentle voice singing O America. America you paradise. America you are cruel. What will happen to my wife, who will feed my little daughters, where did my dreams go? America you are the wind that blew me off your roof, my dreams porcelain shattered into bits.

Thanksgiving Dinner

Sheaves of wheat are centered on the table. My mother's Stradivarius silverware, chosen when she was a young bride years ago because she loved music and ivy china plates only taken out for holiday affairs circle the table. Candles are lit. Every year we get our turkey fresh from the local Gallo Farms, though the duck farms on Long Island have diminished over time. My brother always makes his famous gourmet gravy and every year we tell him he has outdone himself. We guess what secrets are in the stuffing this year. We pass around the sweet potatoes, cranberry sauce and rolls. The turkey is carved. We make a toast, sip some wine, go around the table each one of us reciting what we are thankful for this year. We eat. We compliment the chef, usually my mother. We discuss whether the turkey is the right moistness or not. Looking around the table I see the generations are turning the way the leaves change colors year after year, brown, are raked up and bagged. Grandparents are all gone now. The youngest children are making turkeys by tracing their little hands with a crayon the way I did when I was a child. We make Pilgrim and Indian roly polies year after year. We light the fireplace, roast chestnuts. And then, of course, the pumpkin and apple pies. We gorge ourselves, are happy, contented, ready for the after dinner doze. The phone rings. Usually relatives. My brother answers the phone. He begins chatty then gets quiet. He gets off the phone, turns to us and says "Maff ate a bullet."

The Little Toy Boy

After an afternoon of colors, abstractions, concepts, Minimalism, light shows and imagination galley hopping I walked into the jolting cold air of the outside world. As I continued strolling I found myself near the ramps of the tunnel. Fumes. Dirtiness. Encampments of cars and dumpsters like an encircled wagon train. Fortifications. The Hudson River a Roman Limes. I saw the iridescent swishy tails of the tunnel fish waving at commuter cars. It was then that I saw an older man with a young boy, a halting car, a well attired man inside the car. I saw the frightened big eyes of a little animal as the boy was pushed into the car, money thrown in the direction of the older man. His pimp, I realized. I ran over to the car. "What are you doing?" I screamed. "Where are you taking that child?" The pimp shoved me, ran as the car sped off. Quickly I located a policeman, described what I had witnessed. The policeman inquired if I had gotten the license plate number of the car. No, I hadn't. He told me there was nothing he could do, that perhaps the boy was older than I had thought. I had only recently arrived in New York City. I had never seen a boy prostitute before. Was there more I could have done?

My Mentor, Marsha Tucker*

Meeting Marsha Tucker for the first time I told her how I had demonstrated against the Whitney Museum of American Art. I was in a photo in *Art News* demonstrating because the Whitney wasn't exhibiting very many women artists and had fired Marsha Tucker, the first woman curator ever at the Whitney. Marsha hugged me and hugged me then made a crisscross over her heart and smiled. We were so very different. Marsha was years older than I was, brazen, bold, assertive and Jewish. I was shy, a bit mousy and introverted having been brought up Roman Catholic. Marsha asked me what I did. I told her I was a poet. She hugged me again. She told me how she had met Auden, had several friends who were poets and how she liked to read poetry in her not very often spare time. "Here is my advice to you," she said. "Fail. Fail early. Fail often. Experiment. Fail. Take risks. Fail. Confound. Explore. Fail. Explore some more. Fail. Explore without knowing where you are going, what the outcome in your work will be. Fail. Fall off a cliff. Pick yourself up. Take more risks. Fail. Fail again." "But Marsha," I protested. "I don't want to fail, I want to succeed." "The key to success is failure," Marsha repeated to me with a firm knowing voice. "Fail."

---

*Marsha Tucker was the first woman curator hired at the Whitney Museum of American Art. She was fired from the museum so she decided to found her own museum, The New Museum, NYC.

Debut

At La MaMa E.T.C. on East 4th Street I was waiting for an interview for a poetry reading series. I had never read my poetry out loud in public. When it was my turn I walked in. There was the "mama" of La MaMa, Ellen Stewart. I had brought with me a group of my poems that I believed displayed my range as a poet for her to read. She tossed the white typed on pages aside saying "No. I don't want to read your poems." She looked at me. She stared at me. She walked around me. Sam Shepherd. Andrei Serban. Al Pacino. Some of the famous people she had nurtured. I had been told that mama could smell out talent. It was instinctive with her. "Tell me about your work," she demanded. "It's a theatrical poetry piece built on word associations." "Is it experimental?" she inquired." Yes. Very experimental," I replied. "So experimental that no one is interested in it." She thought for a second then replied "Yes. You will read your theatrical poetry piece." Then she sent me to the stage manager.

"Would you like a podium, chair or will you walk around the stage?" the stage manager asked me. I knew I would be nervous so I asked for a chair. "Center stage or on one side?" "Center." He then set a spotlight on me. It felt hot "Read something." I began reading. "Stop. You have a soft quiet voice. You'll have to read louder." And then again he repeated "LOUDER." I did it. "That's great. And hey —before you go on stage take a swig of brandy. It will relax you."

In the evening at the reading I was sandwiched in between one poet who was a follower of Trotsky and another poet who was a follower of Stalin to help keep them from fighting with each other. I heard my name called. I heard bells. "This is an experimental, theatrical, poetry piece that forms a sliding scale of word associations from ordinary to remote back to ordinary to remote where all the associations are correlated with creativity." I began reading. I read pages and pages of the poem. I felt invigorated. I felt myself floating. I finished with my last line "We are like midwives to a new world being born." A moment of silence. Then the audience clapped and clapped and clapped. Later mama hugged me, said "Very unusual. Creative. Revolutionary." Other people came up to me to congratulate me on my poem. "Experimental," one said. "Extraordinary," said another. I felt flushed, a little tear came to my eye, I took the vow of poetry and I lifted off.

Pamela Rasso grew up in an Italian American family on the Great South Bay on Long Island, NY attending Bellport High School. She continued her education at Nottingham University, England, the State University of New York at Oswego and graduate school at the University of Michigan, Ann Arbor, where she majored in English and writing with a minor in art history writing a master's thesis on the English poet Fulke Greville.

Pamela Rasso is a poet, essayist and film poet. Her poems have been published in many magazines including *The Hiram Poetry Review, Italian Americana, Oberon, The New York Quarterly, Intermuse, Modern Poetry Studies, Mobius: The Poetry Magazine, Gradiva* and *Rattle*. Pamela's collection of poems *The Flickering Locomotive* was a finalist for 4 book competitions.

Pamela's experimental film and video poems include *Transformations, Evocations, A Nuclear Litany, Danae, Spinning Barbie, Anticipating Under Grey Skies* and *Drawn from the Well* which have been shown at art film houses, galleries and festivals.

Pamela Rasso resides in SoHo, NYC with her African Gray Parrot Bazil who recites Shakespeare.

www.ingramcontent.com/pod-product-compliance
Lightning Source LLC
LaVergne TN
LVHW041519070426
835507LV00012B/1694